Over Time

Gavin A. Skerritt

authorHOUSE®

AuthorHouse™
1663 Liberty Drive
Bloomington, IN 47403
www.authorhouse.com
Phone: 1-800-839-8640

First published by AuthorHouse   2/15/2011

ISBN: 978-1-4567-2715-4 (sc)
ISBN: 978-1-4567-2716-1 (e)

Library of Congress Control Number: 2011901058

Printed in the United States of America

Acknowledgements

It's a wonderful feeling to anyone whose family rallies around to support them in whatever they do. For without this support, I may not have had the courage to compile my poems, written over the past eighteen years, to make this book "Over Time".

To my mother (Queenie):

> You always encouraged me though you didn't always understand why or what I wrote. You tried your best with me when I could not express myself. You helped me find this outlet through artistic expression, which eventually led to writing. I remember, sitting privately with you & listening to your comforting words of wisdom on many occasions. Even now, eighteen years later, you're still the mother any son would cherish… & I do cherish you.

To my dad (Bruce):

> Genetics is a powerful thing that is often misunderstood but never questioned. That was what kept us connected! We share the same passion for music, poetry & drawing, and that passion has facilitated my growth to this point. I only hope that this book will help encourage you to follow in my footsteps.

To my beautiful wife (Debbie):

> You've never told me no. You never question why. I acknowledge you because you have always been my best friend since the first day we met. I remember the many nights we stayed up reading poetry until the sun came up. I acknowledge you because you understand that art is expression & nothing else; that it flows through me & not from me. Thank you for believing in me.

To my siblings (Daybal, Dominique & Markus):

> We're really not that different. We just chose to follow different paths. I acknowledge you −− for your respect & love. This book is not just about me & my experiences, but of yours as well.

I acknowledge my Grandparents, aunts & uncles, cousins, step mom, parents-in-law & by best friends. I also acknowledge my University Professor for conditioning me for this first of many publications. He helped me realize that *"once words are written, they no longer belong to you. They belong to the world…"*

You have all inspired me to continue writing, something I've been doing for the past eighteen plus years. You appreciated my love for expression & have supported me even if you didn't quite understand my reasons for doing what I do. So thank you all.

Preface

Poetry, like music, resounds in each & every soul.
It's a painting that that expresses what it sees within itself
& has a burning desire to share with the world.
All YOU have to do is receive it

Artistic expression is a gift that we should all cherish,
for not **everyone has the ability** or the courage **to open themselves up to the world** for critique.

I've been writing poetry for just over eighteen (18) years. But for most of these years these poems were kept private simply because *this* was one of my three outlets within the artistic world from everything happening around me, and I didn't think they were good enough to share. These poems speak of my experiences, specifically about what most people at different points in their lives *think*.

"Over Time" signifies growth. It is a look inside you! In fact, as you read you will notice that "Over Time" my writing style changes as I grow, and so too has my perspective of the world around me.

"Over Time" I hope we all learn to appreciate the pleasures of sharing ourselves with the world around us. For by sharing will only help those around us to grow "Over Time"

Enjoy!

Author's Notes

These poems are a collection of written memories gathered while journeying through life. Growing up in the little Island of St. Kitts, I learned several methods of self-expression, since I was always misunderstood. But writing was the only one (out of music, drawing, painting, and dancing) that soothed my soul to the point where my emotions were captured, but more importantly, controlled. Today I look around and it hurts to see young men who are/were not so lucky to be pointed in a similar direction. But hopefully this will help change that.

As I matured, I learned to develop my gift of writing while living in both Canada & the US – North America. I've come to realize that people live to share their experiences of the world, with the world. After all, history dictates this is how we as human beings have survived for this long! My poetry is simply a list of some of these things. These memories are a collection of thoughts and feelings gathered from the perspective of a growing teenage boy who faces the world as it constantly changes around him. What's so great about this perspective is that you (the reader) have experienced the same things I have and can relate. I am no different from you, nor you from me.

Though I have written close to three hundred poems, I publish only these few thoughts hoping to paint pictures within your minds. Over the years I have watched as each line; as each word creates a separate and distinct picture that most readers can place together to make movies that only they see within their *mind's eyes*. But only if allowed!

I have also learned that most people don't have the capacity to delve within and allow themselves to FEEL. Whether feelings of love, pain, relationships, anger, disgust, life, death... We need to develop the need to feel; to remember. This is how I have learned. This was how I was taught. And this is what I continue to teach. We shouldn't be so numb that we cannot feel what's around us. This numbness is what prevents us from growing "Over Time".

Contents

You surround me...

I left my heart in Barbados

Rain falls like a stagnant hurricane, growing over a single landmass.
Nights as gloomy & cold as a London winter
My mind wanders back to where happiness once roamed free;
The place I left my warm & cozy heart.
No flowers bloom; no sun rises; no birds sing in the space my heart once
     was
And the sound of music, powerless to hypnotize, is but a pleasant
     memory;
Like the heated blood of an old man when he's aroused.

Today I pray I get my heart back.
I need to say
I love you.

You surround me

Starry eyes gaze upon me with the look of innocence.
Everything I've ever known is within your eyes.
So deep is your love; like the ocean blue, filled with everlasting life, never
　　　perishing.

I look back with curiosity,
And I see your untold story.
I love it.

I listen to the voice of your mind through the space between us;
No words spoken, just sighs.
I feel the pleasure that radiates through me from the touch of your skin
　　　when I close my eyes, wishing it were now;
Reminiscing about the scents and tastes of your bodily perfumes.

Imagination keeps you close to me, while lust
penetrates your dark domain in want for me.

Can you feel...?

Can you feel the descent,
entering into you;
my attempts to touch you where
delight and throbbing agony exists in
harmony,
repetitively caressing
your internal desires,
touching your soul?

Can you feel the pulse;
the constant swelling, caused by
amplified heat and pressure generated by
repeated collisions,
the trickle of liquid from opened pores,
the passion that friction causes?

Can you feel the time slipping by,
the changing ambiance within the
vastness of space?

Can you feel the discharge,
my warmth spreading throughout your
bodily hemisphere,
the stiffening of each individual muscle; contractions
produced totally by automatic cognitive reactions to
every twist and vibration your body makes?

Can you feel tranquility and
contentment,
the disappearance of trauma and anxiety
brought forth by world events,
the end of one beginning and the beginning
of another,
the generation of admiration and the desire,

... the love we share?

The Yearning

Just like the Arian Ram that I am,
I'm never easily satisfied
For within my soul lies yearning.
Yearning for something to touch, to feel...
To feel satisfaction?

Something to quiet the raging storms within me,
Something, so I may plant a single seed of affection
That I may watch *it* grow,
And I'll nurture *it*, and care for *it*
That I may watch *it* grow.
It...?

It takes me back to a time when
Hope was once alive, never striving
For survival was easily ascertained
And again I ask, what is this '*it*'?
Is it pain and suffering, or might it be glory
And everything that is good?

Yearning is poisonous to a soul that is insecure
And confused
And poison is not good. Though life is not fair,
Nor death,
Though thoughts are not pure and simple,
And purity does not exist since nothing is everything,
Everything is nothing at all.

You think you see, you imagine you feel
it
but it doesn't even exist within you.

she wandered

she wandered around the room
lost or found?
such grace and confidence
with each perfect step
easily spotted!

she floated near me
poised
such grace and confidence
wandering eyes spoke in tongue
I understood

she sat and wondered why I
stood before her
no intentions
we spoke
she understood

she woke up in my arms
such tenderness
such warmth
such love in her eyes
I understood

she wandered into
St. Kitts...
gratitude
appreciation
was shown

aimlessly, she wandered
within her own mind
I followed
closing distances
she understood

she understood that distance
overwhelming
equates to broken rules
when moon rises
and I rise when my name is called
"Gavinous Ravinous"

wandering spirits search the night
hopes of endless spiritual delight
frozen fingertips reach out
to touch and feel
two souls with zest and zeal
I understand

Dear woman of mine

Scary dreams awaken thoughts
of unwanted possibilities
& time passes by
in slow motion
with control
nonexistent.

Confidence
in ourselves
exist because of
incredible strength,
patience, & belief in God.
To have faith is our only choice.

Just a matter of time

Sittin, chillin, thinkin, contemplatin
Tomorrow…
Growing ever so eager. Growing ever so near
Tomorrow…

Time creeps by, enflaming desires possessed by
Virtuous souls
Tomorrow,
That flame shall grow!

Tomorrow, yearning eyes will glow
Glistening to visions of laughter;
Obvious happiness shall overflow
Tomorrow!

After a wedding

Awaken undaunted soul, caress white sheet with your dark brown skin
- forever a contrast to even my own.
Shower me with passionate kisses; provoke visible thoughts only I can
read.
Part your waves, reveal the life that exists deep within you and let it
overflow...
The depth of your soul I long to touch, to taste and remember forever.

Let memories spark, igniting a flame that keeps expectations soaring
- forever embedded just beyond cognitive reach
Exploration is a constant necessity now, a new language deemed existent
- the sound of breath and wet skin being only a melody that two can
groove to
Just before rhythm is added.

Inhale fragrances that label this meeting erotic, making growth
inevitable.
Lift limbs to accommodate infiltration, guided by palpitating caverns.
Let friction become the main element of raw ecstasy, a pleasurable merger
- a steady, continuous rhythm now created, never to end.
Let time be not a factor for conclusion, nor exhaustion or incompetence.

Ever patient

Raging hormones reek with fine wine & dirty thoughts
But she's not available to me.
My phone is so close & I'm ready for love
& because my appetite for food has diminished, my sexual appetite
Has increased ten-fold.

Raging hormones & swollen pride knock against my body now
But she's not available to me.
What makes it worse is that cold & dampness exists & time is fast
      approaching.
It's almost that time for brown skin to appear once again.
I am overjoyed!

Raging hormones start to cry for time lost can never be regained.
A young man filled with pain sits & writes about it, influenced by falling
      rain.
Although imagination keeps me swollen, & rhythm is maintained
      - mentally
Distance confuses me. I can't refrain.
I need to unleash the dragon.

Raging hormones swell my veins. Yet, I still manage to maintain my
      sanity.
Patiently I wait to share this with her unselfishly, my ever strengthening
      yearning.
My phone is so close & I'm ready for love.
I am overjoyed!
I wait to receive my love from my wife, my ever-lasting love.

Lay with me

I sip while she sings to mellow music
And this melodic sound seeps into my ears.
It was made especially with today in mind!
I pray for comfort & comfort is granted.
And I pray again for company but I'm already forgotten
Perhaps God is still listening but chooses to ignore.
My wife should be here with me.
Listening to the raindrops under my comforter.

Pink treats

I'm thinking of pink treats
Tasty, pink treats
With open lips
Lips that call me
I'm listening to the whispers
Talking back
Maybe I could taste
Hoping I could
Believing its mine to draw close to

Not enough

Another journey begins and I am left staring through my window pain
... again.
A glimpse back in time; harsh reminders; what if's and second-guesses
    Wondering easily becoming excuses for gloomy eyes and misery;
    reasons for sleepless nights and yearning, questioning, confusion.

Possibilities run rampant, and distance needs to be conquered
... yet again.
It is yet to be determined which road is safest
But desire plays a major role throughout my mental journey.

Born to be

Let me be close enough to see my future in your eyes
And forget lost chances and lost love.
Within you lay all possibilities for security.
Nights that rise alongside the sun's rays encourage swollen passages
To connect - with electricity. And time stands still but for a moment
While soldiers roam, searching out their Queen.

Dream with me, a dream that boasts growth and nature;
The result of love between a man and his wife.
For within her now lies the chance to change the world,
Shaping and grooming becoming the main priority.
But now, glowing skin & warm smiles carve pleasant thoughts within my
     mind
Though out of many soldiers, only one remain.

Language and laughter set the sky ablaze
With wishful thinking, now nearing actualization grows upon us.
Keep me close enough to deter harm and negativity
But distant enough for your lungs to breathe that familiar breath.
Your eyes must never lose that glimmer.
I am always here.

Let time sing that familiar song where Holy Grail bears life.
To witness from start to finish, the end of one dream
And the beginning of another; a new chapter in this fairytale, generations
     long.
Tender is a rose petal floating on stagnant water. Let me hold you.
Let me stare and touch and smell all that I've wished for when I asked for
     your mother's hand.
Let me thank God for this opportunity to be your hero.

To gaze upon...

Perfect Sunrise

With the rising of the sun a new hungry dawn arrives;
Its rays unfastens each crease among vast multi-colored blossoms
Across undulating landscape to engulf this vast land.

Awakened, awkward animals in flight soon cast their squawky voices in
      song
To wake sleepy humans & spread life through song.
Then tone-deaf roosters follow out of turn.

Insects crawl through grassy jungles to nourish their young
While avoiding ravenous birds above & below.

Lizards appear, & scurry to gain vantage points so consumption can soon
      begin.

Soldier crabs creep through droopy banana trees; their pace a mad dash
Compared to the snails that attempt to break away from the cold shadows
      of wet rocks.
Only slimy slugs remain.

Sneaky monkeys peep through prickly bush —spying, plotting…
To feed their infants with forbidden fruit, fenced off from predators.

Wild dogs now return to their yards in time to bark,
ready to run away from adventurous intruders.

On the verandah just beyond, cats feverishly lick their tattered body parts
      in silence.

Then surrendered flowers stretch to kiss the sun in pure delight

Lovely morning

Oh what a lovely morning.
The sun is shining,
Birds are flying,
And I have money in my pocket!

11 Moons in my window

I glance through my window at the eight moons above,
Thinking my thoughts and feeling my fears.
The air around me is cool, but comforting –
Never penetrating my black shirt.
The smoke rises slowly from my finger-tips,
Then disappears, much like the supposed troubles I face.

The sounds are peaceful. They skillfully mimic the despair
And hatred I feel all at once, and I hum to myself
Loving the power of self-expression.

Nine moons in my window make me think now
About tomorrow – what's to come?
My memory is fading, much like the smoke from
My finger-tips, into the unknown.

Ten moons in my window make me wonder about
Yesterday and times before,
Of when I tricked myself into thinking I was in love.
And again I move on, knowing I hurt myself
More then I hurt you.
But you can do nothing to help me.

Eleven moons in my window take the place
Of the many stars I neglect to see,
The stars that exist in your eyes and beyond.
And just like the placid air around me, I am
Confronted yet again
Knowing now that I did the right thing
by letting you go.

The Brown Roof

So much depends
upon

a brown shingled
roof

plastered with stuck
sand

over the strong
walls

Inventory of places Propitious for love

There are many.
The weather is always fair, with sunny days all year round.
Weekends invite an eruption of
hormonal dysfunctions –
a venomous toxin
piercing through a sluggish body.
The casting off of its pure light unto
sparkling eyes.
The cool air invites many places:
the beach – any beach,
against the splashing waves,
a hillside,
the back steps
leading to the
verandah
of an old, abandoned hotel room.
Wandering dogs bark, and old ladies peep through
cracked windows.
Car horns wake the dead, and the sound of laughter
creeps through the space where wind usually blows.
Sometimes, the sneaky creeks of boots,
accompanied by a blinding hand-held light
may cause one to pause for a while.
Perhaps one has the option of handling it alone,
of releasing the build-up of stress and discomfort
that lies deep within.
Perhaps idle hands can be put to better use than
just for chores.
Although prevention is better than cure,
I'm not so sure.

Psalms' Replacement

1. The sky is my temple;
    I will not imperil.
2. It encourages me to
    lay down on green hillsides:
    it invites serenity.
3. It relaxes my soul:
    it carries me through the path
    of unconscious desires in
    a dreamy state.
4. Yea, though I float
    through the limitlessness
    of time and space,
    I will not complain:
    for peace is with me;
    its zephyr and moonlit nights,
    they comfort me.
5. It reveals itself to me
    beyond the negativity of my enemies:
    it anoints my mind with purity;
    my head is filled with glee.
6. Surely stillness and tranquility
    will endure within me all the days of my life:
    and I will dwell in the immensity
    of the sky forever.

A Generation

The moss-ridden eerie graveyard replenished thoughts that beneath the earth lay people who cried over death.

Say hello to the moon

Clouds rushing past
        Twinkling streetlamps over a glossy ocean
                Wondering eyes...

Darkness
        Couples
                Yearning eyes...

Dinner by candle light
And lovers locked away in
Pure ecstasy

Gentle breezes and dancing leaves
Sweet embraces and sighs of relief

Now
        Say goodnight...

Her hair

Radiant fleece, flowing unto a charming nape,
Reveals curls not so organized, but instead neglected.
Oh, the joy, filling internal desires tonight,
Awakening vague memories entangled within the bowels of each mind.
I'd rather be free to express myself the way I please!

Sluggish Asia, and scorched Africa...
I once thought them attractive, too far beyond my reach,
Struggling with the conviction of survival at every heart's content.
And though peaceful music radiates throughout my head,
I marvel at your hair, dancing to its rhythm.

Guide me to where men and trees
Depend on each other, where they languish in false victory
Supplied by the sun's harsh rays.
Allow my mind's eyes sail in the vastness
Of your long, flowing braids,

To a place where liquid can quench the thirst
Of my many senses – where peace can find me,
And where ships can be caressed by the black of this ocean's embrace
Against the eternal heat of the sun's rays.
A glorious sky indeed...

Delved into this immense pleasure,
A hidden mass creeps, stalking comfort,
That it may dance to the rhythmic fondling
That creates lethargy and a
Stillness that eases the forever threatening destructive waves.

Blue is the color that masses of follicles create,
Leaving only an immense shadowy canopy.
And I feel, and I examine each one's base,
Gradually becoming mesmerized by the combination of musk,
And tar, and coconut oil. And hours pass me by...

I will reside here, preferably for forever, in that magnificent mane.
I ask, allow my fingertips to create more lavishing braids of
Grandeur? That's all my needy heart desires.
Let me dream, and swim in your ocean of grand design,
And swallow whole the memories that your brilliant mane awakens
        within.

To gaze upon...

Lazy ships lay across gray horizon
Partially filled with the unknown
Red sky denotes unjustified seasonal delinquency
Weather rain or otherwise, unknown

Pondering creative souls sit upon unstable cliff
Staring at water's edge of past & future torture
Dark sky denotes passion & pain
Concentration strictly on the next realistic venture

Preying birds soar against deafening wind
Attention to strategic hunting skills
Hunger, responsibility ever yearning
Internal desires to fulfill

Fiery sun descend behind floating land
Ocean swallowing every colorful morsel 'till total darkness reigns
Un-scattered glistening reflection swaying on stagnant distant seas
Signaling the close to another unperfected day

A child's adoring eyes filled with pure curiosity
That overwhelms and softens already bleeding hearts
Playfulness, daily chores for never ending restlessness
Appreciation for self-expression, a journey through the arts

Not Near

Extended limbs
    Clenching
Shifted shores
    Stifling
Minute granules
    Encouraging
Extended teardrops
    Massaging
Shifted lashes
    Dispersing
Loneliness

Let's sit

Let's sit at cliff's edge
and look toward the
endless blue...
let's talk about
possibilities that exist
there...
that only we can see.
Let's just be...

Let's sit upon a park bench
and smell the roses
blooming in the summer...
let's taste the rain as it drips
from our brows...
and stare endlessly.
Can we?

Let's sit on a crooked porch
and look across the
endless green...
let's feel the cool air after
sunset while staring
at the stars...
I can see...

Lost chances...

Di   "Dee"

I can't believe it.
She gave up, and let me go!
Love, dreams, hopes…
all shattered.
I loved her with all my heart,
and she let me go.

No one ever took the time
to know me and love me like she did.
I took my time,
and grew to love her back.
A strange episode!

We shared everything –
thoughts on life,
thoughts about each other,
thoughts of friendship,
thoughts on trust and love,
and what love should be.

I vowed to only make love
to the one I loved.
I did that, yet after making a fool of myself
just once.

Di was wonderful.
The intense smell of passion
filled the room where emotions overflowed
every time we laid together as one.
Perspiration, tears, saliva and erotic juices,
together in one mixture,
made us one persons for a time.

Time and time again, I begged her
to let me know what was on her mind,
especially if something was bothering her.
That she did, even if I dragged it out of her.
Have faith in me, trust me…
That she did also.
We shared everything between us.
Everything…
…except this!

After seven months, not ten,
my love, my dreams,
our hopes of being together vanished.
She said she was confused.
T'was another who, she said, caught her eye.
Isn't it natural to love another besides your lover?

Trust your heart and your mind as one.
Know where your heart is.
I knew where mine was!

She could not tell me. I guessed it.
Then, she said it.
She lost sleep for a month because of it.
Finally, she asked me to come to her house,
and so I did.
She caressed my face, played with my hair,
and cried.
A lot!
I tried to cheer her up, but she just got more upset.

As I sat, from a drink of water,
I noticed that she was holding a piece of paper.
What was it?

Powerless

dazed & confused, you mumble words of confusion so passionate
yet you comfort me
star-lit nights exist within your eyes, & the world, within your tender
     grasp
you cry like the rain drops that fall upon my window-
     pane
          painful, painless, yet unafraid of the beyond
          confused
so confused am I
for I cannot help you.
distance prevents that
     I know
          I can feel you
so can you feel my anguish
my sorrow
my pain
my false happiness

Lost chances

There were days when the sun seemed
Not to shine,
Nor the wind to blow.
Instead, stillness overwhelmed my being.
Colors were bland; black, white, gray
& never seemed to have desire for change.

Dreary music haunted the air,
Encouraging sleeping dead to lay longer.
Inspiration was non-existent, & trampled roses never bloomed
Facing the sky.
Only one's dreams are comforting...

If Only...

Comfort - externally ascertained
 from unlikely sources.

Watches tick and hands rotate,
yet gridlock presents itself this time.

Drinks are swallowed, tears fall,
& muscular bodies shrivel in despair and punishment.

Weakness is not a physical attribute and
frustration seeps in, for loss is abundantly clear.

Call my name

Alone

                 Sitting

                                Waiting

Call my name

Fans

                 Blowing

                                Hot air

Call my name

Suffocating under the presence of strangers
In a bland terminal
Curious eyes all around
Expensive jewelry
Sweepers
Shopkeepers…

People

                 Walking

                                Watching

I'm not to blame
You know my name?

Wasted time spent with total strangers
Never to be seen again
They never call my name…

Eventually

Eventually dreams are shattered
Eventually goals are attained
And everything seems so insignificant.

Eventually pain and pleasure exist within the same place
- spaces filled with the realization
              That's life!
Eventually

Eventually fallen will rise
Risen will crumble –
Dirt
              Stone
                          Dust
              That's life!
Eventually

Eventually a year becomes a day
- the realization that
Nothing
              Even
                          Matters
Eventually failure itself fails
Uncontrollable circumstances become a place of refuge for the unlikely.
              That's life!
Eventually

Eventually come and go, facing each other, looks exactly the same
From each perspective
Though paths are different, it still remains only one path
- the blind ending a journey whether it be day or night,
Can he see?

Time tells a story for each generation to take heed
No one listens. No one hears.
Eventually.
Roaming spirits sing songs and mortals run scared
Eventually

Nothing
                    Really
                                   Matters
Eventually

Kisses remain

Another Friday, & again I'm
Sitting here wondering what's there to do...
Where should I go?

Youthful lies of tales being whispered
Into mature ears, eyes seeing
Ever so clearly.

Long distances overcome, issues
Not problems! Satisfaction becomes found once again
Through glassy eyes & sweet kisses.

Again, youthful lies...
& long distances become longer through yearning & wishing.
Only memories of sweet kisses remain.

Downfall

Disgruntled and unsatisfied.
Denied compensation. No relaxation.
Imagination forced into stagnation.
Terrorizing my generation throughout this nation.
Probation that lacks fair consideration.
Self-preservation?
Imagination's sublime creation!

Chance — answer to "Truth"

To seek the truth is but a chance
- a journey less traveled by those who fear life.
Time is no factor where failure is always a possibility
- again a journey, but less traveled by fear itself.
Doubt & desperation will always be a contradiction!

What's the difference between now & then?
Time...
> The cycle grows over time, truth known only to those involved.

Perception is swayed only by those who either rush or wait.
> Even then only time dictates which will exist & when.

Lost & found are more alike than you think – perception...
I am *lost* in this love I've *found*. Accidents do happen!
We learn, we aspire, we discover.
Truth lies not with one's destination,
But along a path that only time can pave...

Broken Promises

Time sneaks around pretending to care about unknown outcomes;
Raising hopes flushed with desire & life.
A lonely bedside so cold echoes your name while pleasant dreams take
    place.
You are for now a memory, a reminder of things to come.

Wandering to familiar places that seem new is yet more punishment for
    even the strongest mortal when reality hits. And it hurts.
One tries to forget pain, but pain arises to squeeze & grind one against a
    wall of depression over & over & over... to be trampled repeatedly.

Disappointment is a harsh reality that many embrace as such - God's
    predestined course has already been charted... or so is believed -
    Forever a controversy against free will.
Light showers become heavy balls of hail that pound against panes of
    glass.
I can no longer sleep. It hurts that I can't see you just because I'm not
    allowed to.

Intoxicated

It sailed across a restless tongue, now tasteless
blood from a tilted glass,
provoking emotional despairs in lonely souls.

Blurred vision & distorted sounds tell one lie after another
but I'm still focused.
I can see you clearly!

It is a comforting smell that does bodily damage.
And again, I'm caught lying to myself
laying in wait for your arrival

But you never come

If only

Passion withheld and chances lost.

Curious gazes filled with good intentions.

Touches never known.

Dreams never realized.

Patience, a forced reality...

Time, a curse that cannot be broken...

Steps taken that won't be retraced.

The absence of self actualization prolonging what could be, or what will?

Proximity against two souls for eternity.

Convenience... safety first!

Complicated but not impossible; eyes remain wide open

Time and time again

Beneath the sun I cast scattered seeds of dreams
Hoping that at least one will find soil
Under this sea of pavement
A vision not to rule the world but to influence those who inhabit it.
They drown in sorrow, pain, despair, selfishness and their own ignorance
Haphazardness is the order of the day
And as usual I witness constant destruction as seeds are unknowingly
    crushed
Time and time again.

Blindness is not only for those who cannot see
But for those who refuse to acknowledge their next steps
Before the next teardrop hits
Life's lesson is a river filled with the constant struggle to shun insanity
But the sane are never revealed at face value
And growth is imminent when kicked, not crushed
For not too long from now even on pavement my seeds will grow
Time and time again.

Pressing on...

One in the same

Perched on the verandah, you & I,
Words flow
From our hearts, our minds.
Personalities are similar, though we exist in
Separate words.
Love is the same.

Good & bad exists within
The same space,
That we understand.
Accept it we must.

How did I get here?
Why am I here?
Thinking – protect you I must, from yourself,
From me, from the world & everything in it?

So we ponder, perched on the verandah
& words flow.
From our hearts, our mind
Questions persist.
Accept it we must,
For love is the same.

Lost note from a simple song

He was no mentor,
encouraged confrontation, performances, self expression.
Tried to show his sensitivity.

His mirrored image roamed the streets at night,
miserable, almost dead.
Yet showed no hints outright.

That face, expressionless, hid pain well.
Delight and satisfaction seemed to exist
until separation proved otherwise.

Endless compassion never seemed to penetrate,
tears, words and piercing stares, perspiration,
frightfully, from the voice of harmonic keys:

It seems ironic,
now that independence is proven, there is no note
with which to make music.

That thing

It grows
Long & thick,
Ever expanding.
It raises brows, either in delight
Or disgust
& causes the expansion of pupils
In awe.

From a stubble
It grows,
Filling every inch of space it glides past
Ever so slowly.
From the breaking of one's skin,
It curves, conforming to each
& every gap it penetrates.

Size, length, & even thickness varies,
For genetics dictates this!

Toy's Plea

Opportunities taken that satisfy
Cries of emotion
Run rampant
When outcomes remain unknown and
Internal confusion induces stress
And questions are asked
- Confusion

Written words translating
To fallen tears
And happiness lasts until the
Applause is over.
Then people talk,
Knowing only their simple pleasures
Yet mine remain unresolved.

Guarantees of accomplishments
Remain congested in the hands of
The world around me;
People I've never seen or heard.

He is out there.
Depressed,
Un-forgiven in my time of need.
When will he arrive
To share in this timeless bliss?
Contradictory, endless, yet non-existent bliss.
I need to share myself as I see fit!
I sing cries of love for you
My love,
My ever-lasting love...

Pressing on

Awaken my child from sleepless slumber
Dive into the depths of your own well of despair
Climb down towards hellish dreams and distasteful possibilities
Recover your own essence. Re-discover your own fantasies.

Tread meticulously, carefully. Look around. Remember!
Remember when you smiled, and I smiled back
Remember the experiences that made you you
Remember to never forget. You are who you are!

Once upon a time, you didn't care for subtle steps or cautious measures
Your automatically retained strength was constantly regenerated and
Issues were forthright challenges, not problems.

Through you...

when words are spoken, feelings are shown...
  sometimes
when eyes meet & hands caress
steady heartbeats become duress...
  sometimes
sublime desires birth new realities
for those who yearn for comfort, though
  sometimes
death occurs; they say it makes us stronger...
  sometimes

To behold...

The world, seen through the eyes of one so beautiful,
Is not so bleak
And extended self, comprising of all that is visually lovely to behold,
Is flush with purity.

Wonder & magnificence, the very essence of human existence,
Overwhelms even the most gracious
Yet initiates increasing growth of imagination of some, sometimes
Never to be seen by another.

Silent night, filled with absolutely nothing,
Is indeed filled with peace
- Just like the stare of an infant, though pouring rain
Crashes against galvanized roof.

Stretching upward, outward, toward unknown possibilities,
Is not so bleak
And dreams fulfilled, an extension of one's self,
Will reach the deaf and blind.

In Time

Flatter me, but never lie.
I know that time heals.
But why wait, when now is just as good a time as any?
To procrastinate is every dreamer's desire
Not to feel feelings now. But in time, they will!

"In time," they always say, "hearts will heal...
Truth, be revealed. You will love again."
But what is there to love, if not have passion for?
Pain still hurts, cuts still bleed, and scars will always remain.
Time makes no difference!

Make hay. Don't tell me about Rome.
Patience cannot be manufactured.
Plan... execute... follow through
Three keys to human evolution, 'till now.
To seize the moment in time will forever remain a contradiction!

Pressing On

Time is a living space
With endless possibilities
And vast colors
And boundless lengths
And limitless visions

Like you

Time asks for nothing
But for honesty
And individualism
And responsibility
And devotion

To reside

Time waits for nothing
Not necessarily impatient
And incognizant
And unforgiving
And close-minded

It's reality

Proposal

Confidence sometimes exists when one grows tired of waiting, of hoping,
Then grows 'till necessity overpowers lust,
But remains identical.

Comfortable?

Make me believe

Tell me anything.
Satisfy your desire to please me.
Lie just once more.

Take advantage.
Please make me smile right now.
Just tell me anything.

Be deceitful.
Body language & glaring eyes...
Keep practicing.

Sell

Gentle prospect
wondering what's next
let me steer you where you need to go.
You don't know it yet, but you want what I have!

Step and ponder in my direction
Glance into my eyes
Let me approach you – because you need my guidance.
You don't know it yet, but I already know what you're looking for!

Turn and gaze;
show me those gleaming eyes
Listen to my enchanting voice – because you are curious.

By now, the music you hear has worn you down
and dimmed lights wash speculation out the door;
the aroma fills your body with a sense of belonging.
It regenerates you and is transformed into words proving captivation.

Sighs and smiles
emerging from dead depths...
let me help you take your bag before you realize what just happened.
You don't know it, but my commission check just grew even more!
Just one meal

Another day to think
With past similes behind her
And though considered an attitude
        Happiness has escaped her

Slumber beckons for obedience
And so does the need for nourishment
But comfort beneath these warm cotton sheets will win this day
        So to God she prayed

Eyes closed tight and it feels right that she might
Not move, but for position to watch rays pierce through seeing blinds
Light blinding, wind whistling, sounds resounding
    Yes she's listening

Bathroom break? Now she takes a chance to make
Her stomach stop growling before she realizes
Its now night. There's no light, no sound, no warmth beside her being
    So she starts eating

Down

Bed so cozy, keep me close. Wrap me in your tender loins.
You are my only comfort now.
Erase the sunlight from my window pane and let everlasting darkness
    reign
-A wish I make in moment's silence.

I'd rather lay here with eyes closed, ignoring the world and all its troubles
Than face it head on.
I'd rather lay here speechless, thinking nothing but what I don't have
Than attain what I dream of constantly.

No voice of reason can penetrate. No praise, no eagerness, no
    compliment.
Right now I see the world and everything in it as a plot to drown me in
    my own sorrow
And I want it to!
So please forgive me for ignoring you…

Sometimes I lay awake with my eyes closed tight, wishing I was dead.
But death ignores me.
Sometimes I even hear it laughing at me with a chorus, loud and clear,
    often very appealing.
And I'd rather not acknowledge it with a smile.

To stare at the ceiling above has now become a norm; a necessity.
I float with intensity, looking down upon my lifeless body;
Mirrored image revealed in thin air.
Please hold me close.

Why now does noise bellow for me to raise my glass stained with blood?
A bottle whispers my name as I walk away.
It seems I am popular among vintage, tasteless, blurry blissful fantasies.
To be awake reveals constant pain and suffering. Yet still I swallow.

Don't call my name, don't say a prayer, don't utter one word.
I will try my best to ignore you.
Let me wallow in self-pity. Ignore me. Let me be. Leave me alone, please.
I still wish for total silence.

Don't sleep too long...

Office excitement

It's too quiet and I'm bored
And words dance around inside my head
Responsibilities fulfilled
Makes the man behind the glass smile.
And the radio sings to me,
Expressing words of pain and suffering.
It ends.
It's too quiet and I'm bored.

Faint sounds of political issues
Struggle to turn sharp corners and travel long distances
Knocking on the drum
Buried inside my head.
Distasteful, inaccurate,
Boring words.

Time well wasted

Inspiration is lacking in the mind of a creator.
Expression evades him artistically.
A vast liquid space clouds judgment.
Familiar sources are nowhere to be found.
He lays searching in an unconscious state.
He hopes to catch a glimpse of a single syllable
To spark into a burning spear of fruition
That shuttles one to blissful conclusions
While searching in his ocean of memories
Only to be greeted by the endless shore of refusal

near arrival

with each seed planted
growth is expected
& unexplained euphoric sensation
turns to pure unadulterated panic

Hi Expectations

You make it hard to be the man I ache to become
With *your* dependence and trust in what
I can't seem to see within myself.
But *you* have undying faith.
This image *you* gaze upon is what brought *you* here
– imagination pregnant with false security, but *you* still believe.
I'm mystified; this mirror does not reveal to me what *you* repeatedly speak
    of!
So instead I blame *you* for my short-comings, so uncomplicated
- there is no one else to blame. Not even me.
My weak attempt to bear the burden of manhood has disheartened me
And my exploration to preserve my sanity has approached extermination.
So instead:

-    The sun never touches my pale skin.

-    Only the simple courtesies are extended.

-    Bed linen grows on me like skin.

-    Communication is withdrawn

But *you* never stray…
Your undying faith in love remains

Introduction to my first born

I saw you when you weren't even looking.
Your eyes were sealed shut,
Not by the tiny lids that protect them
Or your tiny hands that covered them,
But by your mother's exposed skin.
And although you didn't know
Your knees from your elbow
You smiled at me
As if you saw me smiling back.
You twisted & turned, & made a faint sound
All inside your shielding sack

Touch me

Secretly a bellow resonates silently
Across incomprehensible distances,
No voice heard.
    Cerebral connection established.
    Absence of yesterday.
    Memento of precedence.
Spawn's ignorance linger
While thoughts detained remain sustained.
Only restraint.

Don't sleep too long

You lay on new linen
shrouded with the stain of rotting skin
for the world to see
The memories distorted like dizziness
A cold, cold breeze rebounds from your face
like the painful image that makes loved ones weep

Don't sleep too long.
Medication awaits with eagerness to heal
arteries that form boundless pressure within you
-    a son & daughters insistence with *Grand* designs

-    a parent's love

-    and countless possibilities

Wake to sing a choir's song, in reverence.
No need to wait for Sunday morn'
so far away
Your breath wrapped & placed in a box
Eyes witness closing with vivid non-acceptance
Tear, dirt, stares

He sees me

He sees through me with glazed, preset eyes
And never says a word.
His actions would speak louder if not for pure mystification
Totally misconstrued.
Yet time after time
    He sits
    He stands
    He lays
    He leans...

He sees through me and never says a word.
A man, usually filled with pure emotion
Sits empty and bare
Empty and bare
He sits empty and bare

He sees through me and never says a word.
Every change in me discovered in an instant
His eyes tell a confusing tale, only to be assumed
Then *he* slowly walks away
He simply walks away

He sees through me and never says a word.
Laying in wait. Listening. Watching. Staring.
At least *he* acknowledges me
Because I know him distinctly
He lays silently waiting

He sees through me and never says a word.
He sees my discontent, my anguish, my assumed failed
    attempts
He acknowledges me
Because *he* sees me
I know *he* sees me

Lightning Source UK Ltd.
Milton Keynes UK
172899UK00002B/211/P